This book is dedicated to my father and mother. I am nothing without their love and support...

HUMANISTIC ASPECTS IN THE SELECT NOVELS OF MULK RAJ ANAND

MRS. J. MERCY RANI MRS. RUFINA ROSLIN MARY

Contents

About The Author

Ms. J Mercy Rani is a faculty of English at Nehru Arts and science College, Coimbatore. She is a teacher, reader, guide and motivator. She completed her graduation in coimbatore, Tamilnadu. Having worked in various institutions for more than 10 years, she has a vast knowledge on English Literature and Language. She has passion towards teaching Literature among young graduates. She spends most of her time reading, cooking, traveling and visiting places. She has published papers in National conference.

Mrs. Rufina Roslin Mary is working as an Assistant Professor of English in Nehru Arts and science College, Coimbatore. She is a passionate in teaching English Literature. She loves reading, analysing and discussing crime thriller and detective novels. She has more than 10 years of experience and presented papers in National conference.

CHAPTER ONE

Introduction

The place of English in the whole scheme of our education has been a subject of much heated debate. English is a foreign language. A foreign language, like a foreign plant, can grow with great difficulty in a foreign soil. It is a hard task to master it. In spite of all this, we are ardent admirers of English. English education has admittedly done us great good. Though English cannot be the medium of instruction its study is both a necessity and an advantage. It is one of the richest languages in the world, in respect of literature and culture.

English language has given rise to great social ideas and great political ideas. The seed of Indian writing in English was sown during the period of the British rule in India. Now it has blossomed into an evergreen tree. The products of Indian writing are being read and assimilated by not only the native people, but by the foreigners also. It has happened after the tremendous and constant efforts that have been put by novelists like Aurobindo, R.K. Narayan and Raja Rao. In the modern age it is being popularized by a number of writers and has won accolades all over the world.

Srinivasa Iyengar says, "One touch of nature makes the whole world kin, but it is in literature that the heart-beats of a nation are heard" (Indian Writing in English, 1). In the earlier years Indian Writing in English is known as Indo-Anglian literature. It is legitimate to view Indo -Anglian literature as a curious native eruption, an expression of the practical no less than creative genius of the Indian people. Indian writing in English achieves self expression too artistically using English in its own way. The Indo- Anglian literature is different from the Anglo-Indian literature. The former is the genre written and created by the Indian through the English language and the latter is written by the Englishmen on themes and subjects related to India. Racial and Political tensions are a constant theme of Indo -Anglian literature and it can be seen in E.M. Forster's *A Passage to India* (1924).

"The novel by definition – is a very loose genre, almost elusive to the critics' attempt at categorizing and systematizing it that abstract consideration here will, by necessity, be restricted to the barely essential", says Dhawan (Common Wealth Fiction, 49). The rise of the novel in India is associated with the socio-political-economic conditions. The appearance of the novel synchronized with the rise of individualism and with all the consequent political and social reorientations, which followed.

The birth of the novel took place in Bengal like the birth of prose. Bankim Chandra Chatterjee established the novel as a major literary form in India. Ramamurthy says that "It was he who showed that the ordinary life of the middle class Bengali could be the subject matter of a high class novel and the religious and social views could be put across through artistic merits" (Rise of the Indian Novel in English, 38-39). Bankim Chandra Chatterjee was a superb story teller. Though he was the first Indian to write a novel in English, he wrote fiction only in Bengali. However, he was a true pioneer of the Indian novel in English.

Indian English literature is an honest enterprise to demonstrate the ever rare gems of Indian writing in English. Rather than from being a singular and exceptional, Indian writing in English has turned out to be a new form of Indian culture and voice in which India converses regularly. Indian writers, poets, novelists, essayists and dramatists have been making momentous and considerable contributions to world literature. Since pre-independence era, the past few years have witnessed a lot of prosperity and success of Indian English writing in the global market.

Indian writing in English has attained an independent status in the realm of world literature. Wide ranges of themes are dealt within. Recent English fiction has been trying to give expression to the Indian experience of the modern predicament. There are a many critics or commentators in England and America who appreciate Indian English works.

India has a deeply established and developed literary scene of writing in English in comparison to other countries of erstwhile British colonial rule. Global economic prominence has inspired a fast-changing literary scene. These literary developments are impacting not only Indian writing in English within India but also the genre, forms, voices and modes of artists' expression, engaged with representing this emerging economy.

The freedom struggle awakened the Indians who sought to gain freedom from the torturous regime of the British. The writers were also able to propagate their point of view, which ultimately helped to motivate and guide the masses. The horrors, tragic consequences and partition like the large scale migration, reckless looting and merciless massacres were portrayed by the writers in their works which captured the interest, and imagination of the readers. The Indian English works began to prove its mark in the global literary scenario. East–West conflict, multi-culturalism, social realism, gender issues, comic aspect of human nature, ecological concerns, magic realism, diasporic writings and the like became the themes of the post independent writers.

English has acquired rare privilege popularity in India especially among the elite and the middle classes. It is increasingly used by writers to give shape to the conflicting dilemmas and issues that confront the human psyche. The Indian English writers use English with a lot of ease and it has become a convenient medium to express the intrinsic talents of the writers.

Indian writing in English has acquired fame and administration in both India and abroad. It is now in its full swing. The works of the Indian writers of English are not an imitation of English literary patterns but highly original and intensely Indian in both theme and spirit. They have given new shape to the English literature.

The Indian English fiction has made a lot of growth during the dawn of the millennium years and the writing in all genres of literature has gained momentum, particularly the Indian novel Dozens of the Indian writers like R.K. Narayan, Mulk Raj Anand and their like promoted the conventional mode of writing. The crusaders of the contemporary and modern era included Salman Rushdie, Amitav Ghosh, Vikram Seth and many more. They substantiate the strength of the emerging modern India. A host of contemporary post-colonial writers like Salman Rushdie, Arundati Roy, Meera Alexander, Anita Nair, and Jhumpa Lahiri have initiated the process of decolonizing the "colonial English" and using it as a medium to express Indian thoughts and sensibilities with a distinctive Indian style.

Indian fiction in English can be divided into three phases. The first began in the 1850's and ended in 1930. Writing in this period was romantic and historical and often dealt with India's potential freedom. Attitudes of the Indians were also changing. From frustration and feelings of inferiority, Indians developed a new sense of self –awareness and Sri. Aurobindo Ghose belongs to this phase.

The second phase (1930's to 1970's) began when the Civil Disobedience Movement led by Mahatma Gandhi was launched in India and a national consciousness was awakened. The freedom movements led by Gandhi created a lot of activity in the literary world. The need for an autonomous, independent country led to an explosion of creativity. It encouraged the masses to wipe out the British from the Indian soil. Therefore, there was a flourishing of novels in both regional and national stream. This burst of energy in regional literature, laid the ground work of enhancing the vibrancy and the scope of the Indian English fiction.

The dual combination of independent movement and nationalist consciousness led to the out flow of novels in which affection for motherland was the basic theme and this seemed to invoke the patriotic sentiments of the masses, Raja Rao's novels like *Kanthapura* (1938) and Mulk Raj Anand's *Untouchable* (1936) revolved around the varying themes of the independence struggle. Post – independent India also produced a number of novels involving the aftermaths of the freedom movements.

The triumvirs Mulk Raj Anand, Raja Rao and R.K. Narayan were the novelists who stabilized and fortified the Indian English fiction with their sample works and unique literary style. The three novelists enjoy a unique position in the literary scene of Indian fiction. Anand's Novels (1950 – 2000) brought to picture the inequalities of the society and the trials and tribulations of the less fortunate. "Mulk Raj Anand's novels constituted a considerable breakthrough in Indo Anglican literature by indicating the wealth of material in the life of India's 'downtrodden masses' and in the drama of revolutionary nationalism available to novelists of combining social realism with fervent didactism" (Indo Anglican Literature a Survey, 5). R.K. Narayan (1906 – 2001) is another celebrity, who is undoubtedly the masters of portraying the socio – economic aspects of the ordinary Indian's family, Raja Rao's (1908-2006) reputation as a novelist of metaphysics and philosophy is justified by his contribution in upholding these themes in his novels.

The final phase of Indo Anglian writing began in the 1970's within the state of emergency declared by the late Prime Minister Mrs. Indira Gandhi and continues today. Writers displayed an increasing freedom with language, fantasy, irony and satire.

The creative writing in the eighties transcends the East-west conflict and portrays the new post colonial India within its evolving outlook, which is a blend of tradition and modernism. It depicts the cosmopolitan outlook of the new generation who strives to strike a balance between the inherited traditional values and the imbibed foreign culture. The treatment and technique of the novel is transnational and transcontinental. Salman Rushdie, Amitav Ghosh and Upamanya Chatterjee have made bold attempts to recapture the altered perceptions of post-colonial India and the use of narrative technique has elevated their position among the writers of Indian fiction in English.

Some of the best studies of social life are, naturally enough in the regional languages. Urban life in India attracts the novelists by its excitement, perversions and sophistications but the interior, the areas of obscurity and inaccessibility have their attractions too, and sometimes bring out the best in the creative novelist.

Women novelists have played a crucial and momentous role in enhancing the quality and quantity of the Indian English Fiction. They have further added the women's feministic dimensions to the novels. In the past, the works by the Indian women authors have always been undervalued due to some patriarchal assumptions. Indian societies gave priorities to the works of male experiences. In those days women used to write about women's perception and experiences within the enclosed domestic area. Male authors used to deal with heavy themes. So it was assumed that their work would get more priority and acceptance in the society.

In the 19th century, more and more women actively participated in India's reformist movement against the British rule which led to women's literature. The contributions by women writers cannot go unnoticed. The works by women writers comprise a major part of the contemporary Indian writing in English. Today women are seen establishing their identity in almost all walks of life. They have heralded a new consciousness in the realm of literature also.

Women Novelists from a class apart, since they have developed their own styles which expresses feminine sensibility. Kamala Markandaya, Ruth P. Jhabvala, Attia Hussain, Anita Desai, Santha Rama Rao, Kamala Das, Shashi Despande, Bharati Mukherjee and Prema Nandakumar were some of the most famous novelists. Shobha De, a staunch expert of women empowerment recognized the displacement and marginalization of women in India.

Among the women writers Sarojini Naidu, charmed the readers with her writings. Feministic themes have also been used by authors, like Nayantara Sahgal and Rama Mehta. Regional fictional themes have been aptly used by Kamala Das, Anita Desai and Susan Viswanathan. Novelists like Anita Desai and Kamala Markandaya captured the spirit of Indian cultures and its traditional values. During 1990's India became a popular literary nation as a number of women writers made their achievement in this era. Most of these female novelists are known for their bold views that are reflected in their novels.

In the 20th century women's writing was considered as a powerful medium of modernism. The last two decades have witnessed a lot of success in feminist writings. Today the categories of those women writers who have money and western education have gained prominence. They describe true and whole world of women frankly in their writings. The majority of these novels depict the psychological sufferings of the house wife. Virginia wolf's contribution in this field is significant.

Since long, feminism has been used by the women novelists. These novels reflect the ability and competence of women in the present age. Indian women writers explore the feminine subjectivity and apply the themes ranging from childhood to complete childhood.

Indian women writers like Kamala Markandaya, Bharati Mukherjee, Anita Desai and many more have played an important role in conveying a wide range of Indian issues to the readers. This new voice of emerging novelists have succeeded in drawing the attention of the public towards the problems of gender inequality, social evils and exploitation of women in a patriarchal society. Kamala Markandaya (1921 – 2001) explores a multitude of issues and the choice of themes made her approach the subject with proper organization. The popularity of Kamala is based on her short studies and autobiography. Anita Desai has focused on the lives of women played with troubles in a male dominated society in her novels. Bharati Mukerjee, the expatriate of the Indian origin in the U.S.A., Shashi Despundle and Geeta Hariharen (1954) are other remarkable writers who have contributed a lot in fiction of the post-modernist literature.

The prominent make fiction writers of this era are not large in numbers. Sparking writers is Sudhin N. Ghose with his two books *And Gazettes Leaping, Cradle of True Clouds(1951)* and *Varmitlion Boat(1954). And Gazettes Leaping* has been highly admired by one and all. The other fiction writer is Ruskin Bond, who wrote his first novel *The Room on the roof* at the age of seventeen. It was awarded the John Lewellyn Rhyz Prize in 1957. He is a man of fantasy.

In the post – independence era, the Indo Anglian writers of fiction are more self-confident than ever before. There is a sudden widening of the horizons and a keener and deeper interest in the history of our people and country. There is a conflict of ideologies ranging in the minds of our post-independence novelists. Whereas poverty, hunger, death, and disease form the key-notes of the symphony, movements like humanitarianism, socialism and liberalism would influence their writings in the near future.

The importance of Indo -Anglian fiction has been recognized. Many good Indo Anglian novels and many more short stories have demonstrated the feasibility of the Indians writing fiction. There is a great hurdle as the unique intricacies of social life and the untranslatable nuances of conversation speech are better rendered through the medium of one's own mother–tongue. But the creative Indian fiction writers have overcome this problem. Much creative work in fiction has been done in English. Several good novels and short stories have appeared either as translations as original works. In the present century fiction in English has been attempted which has borne rich fruit.

A pioneer of Indian writing in English, Mulk Raj Anand is the best known writer of the Indian fiction of the 1930s. He gained an international recognition early in his life. He was a founding member of Progressive Writers Association, a National Level organization that wielded considerable influence during India's freedom struggle and beyond. An incredibly prolific writer, Anand's creative career spanning a period of more than seventy five years has been intertwined with the search for a just, equitable and formed looking India. He has written extensively in areas as variegated and diverse as art and sculpture, politics, Indian literature and history of ideas. The library of congress has more than one hundred and fifty publications by him in its collection. Sahitya Akademi Award, "Padma Bhushan" and Leverhulme Fellowship are some of the awards and accolade that he won during his long literary career.

He was notable for his depiction of the lives of the poorer castes in traditional Indian society. One of the pioneers of Indo- Anglian fiction, he with R.K. Narayan, Ahmed Ali and Raja Rao was one of the first India based writers to gain an international readership. He was the most prolific of his contemporaries and his literary works include about twenty five novels, a few collections of short stories and numerous non-short fictional works. His life and achievement include a variety of fields, fiction, journalism, editorship, politics, social welfare and administration. His most ambitions mode of expression has been fiction.

A versatile genius, a humanist an optimist, an able speaker and organizer, a literary architect – all in unique is Dr. Mulk Raj Anand. He has brought the form of novel in line with the latest development in Indian writing in English today. The selection of his novels has been done keeping in mind social heredity or the civil of casteism, environment and his brand of humanism which make his final pronouncement on mankind.

He preaches as Sorokin advocates in his *Reconstruction of Humanity* that man should acquire spiritual awareness and altruism for the welfare of humanity and should cease his onslaught of humanity. To expand his philosophy, Anand has aptly opted fiction as his mouthpiece. In his novels, it is mainly man's cruelty to man that he describes and affectively evokes our sympathy and compassion. His personal experiences and the reform of Indian's political social and cultural institutions are the major elements in Anand's writings.

He is considered by many critics to be one of Indian's best writers and is often described as the "father of Indo-Anglian Literature" along with R.K. Narayan and Raja Rao, he established the basic forms and themes of Indian Literature that is written in English. Anand is not only a writer, art critic and philosopher but also an active fighter for the modern humanist movement in India. His humanity and curiosity place him among the leading novelists of the current age. He has contributed new techniques, new subject matters, new approaches and new styles. His literary career is based both in India, England and other countries. His contribution to the preservation and promotion of Indian Art is equally significant and Marg, a magazine dedicated to revealing lesser known facts of the world of art, will remain a lasting testimony to this.

Though historically Indian English fiction owns its origin to Bankim Chandra Chatterjee's *Raj Mohan's Wife* (1864), its foundation was laid by Mulk Raj Anand when he published his *Untouchable* in 1935. Mulk Raj Anand, R.K. Narayan and Raja Rao have broken new grounds in Indian English fiction in terms of making innovations in themes and techniques.

He was among the first writers to incorporate Punjabi and Hindustani idioms into English. His stories depict realistic and sympathetic portrait of the poor in India.

He is regarded as one of the founding fathers of English fiction. He has brought innovations in fiction by making an untouchable the hero or the anti-hero of his first novel, *Untouchable.*

The social heredity of caste system cannot be altered and passes from the parents into their progeny as a socio-psychological inheritance. The caste system is usually characterized by hierarchies whose members have hereditary professions and are segregated strictly by rules restricting social interchange to persons of the same caste. The Brahmin priests are considered as the holders of maximum purity, are the top of the system. The untouchables, the holders of maximum impurity are at the bottom.

While social heredity is an entirely indigenous phenomenon in our country, the social environment has universal dimensions. The social environment in which a person lives influences his life to a great extent. No man can escape from the social environment in which he lives. The influence of the environment conditions on human beings is so amazing that sometimes, it finally leads him to his destiny. To a large extent, our habits, words, thoughts, our aspirations and our lives depend upon the social environment and society that surround us. The conditions of social environment in which we spend our lives have a great influence upon the minds and morals of man which ultimately shapes our destinies. Cassier elucidates the point "Man like animals submits to the rulers of society but in addition, he has an active power to change the form of social Life." (FLNHH, 90).

Our present study is to find out the humanistic aspects in the novels of Mulk Raj Anand, who is the best known writers of the Indian fiction of the 1930's. Anand has shown his contempt for all kinds of exploitations in the modern society. He strongly condemns the cruelty and the pain inflicted upon the underprivileged by the higher sections of the society.

Three novels *Untouchable, Coolie* and *Two Leaves and a Bud* have been selected for the study which brings out the humanism of Anand at its best. Our study is concerned with penetrating deep into these three novels and finding out the extent of Anand's humanism.

The second chapter deals with Anand's first novel *Untouchable* (1935). The chapter clearly indicates the social heredity of caste system which becomes a great catalyst in the development of man and shapes his destiny.

This chapter deals with the problems faced by the untouchables and women, created by the dominant people, right from independence to the present era. The wealthy people live a prosperous life by the manual labour and toil of the untouchables. The untouchables are seen as permanent pollutants, an assumption which is frequently based on the special nature of their hereditary professions.

Anand's concern for the downtrodden and the oppressed is revealed here. The novel describes a child of modern India shackled by the age-old tradition and Bakha is a perfect individual whose excellence is flawed by his low-caste for which he is not responsible. Bakha was aware of the limitations of the given social structure. He is defeated between the struggle of the individual and the society.

While social heredity is an entirely indigenous phenomenon in our country, the social environment has universal dimensions. The following chapter deals with the influence of the environmental conditions on the lives of human beings.

Coolie(1936) is a story of Munoo, whose life is determined by the social forces. He is a fifteen year old boy who has to work as a child labourer and eventually dies of tuberculosis. The novel takes us to different places and cities showing the inhuman and degrading treatment shown to the coolies. Anand was able to strike a chord in the beautiful and real to life portrayal of the down trodden masses of Indian Society, the so called have nots. The humanism of Anand is finally depicted in his chapters. He has made a sincere and intense effort to promote the welfare and happiness of those who are treated unjustly by the majority of people for one reason or another.

Anand while emphasizing the determinism of social environment in *Coolie* (1936) traverses it in an arch. The protagonist of the novel moves from the village to town, from the town to the city and then up to the mountains and is finally swept away to his doom.

No man can escape from the social environment in which he lives. The influence of the environmental conditions on human beings is so amazing that it finally leads him to his destiny. To a large extent, the conditions of social environment in which man lives have a great influence upon our minds and morals which ultimately shape our destinies.

The influence of the social environment on the lives of man also finds expression in Anand's novel *Two Leaves and a Bud*. Here also his humanism is being described in full swing. The fourth chapter deals with Anand's *Two Leaves and a Bud*. It designates the tragic journey of Gangu - the protagonist from a village in Punjab to the naturally beautiful Assam. It deals with the suffering and misery of the workers on the tea plantations of Assam. Here Anand has delineated the lives and experiences of the millions of people living in an alien society.

He has brought a creative humanism to bear upon his works; Anand upholds humanism as his philosophy of life and makes his fictional creations as instruments of humanism. He made the assertion that in humanism man is the most important factor.

In this chapter Anand has given a real picture of the depravity caused by imperialism on all fronts. The dehumanizing role of the British in India, the injustice of the British Raj, the exploitation of the Colonialists and the suffering of the Indian masses is exposed in this novel.

The protagonists drawn from the oppressed classes are simple, innocent, intellectually undeveloped though only faintly aware of the nature of the social forces working against them. Probing into the minds of the characters, Anand brings out what is essentially human in them, fusing the inner psychological problem with the outer reality. Gangu in *Two leaves and a Bud* suffers and becomes a passive victim of social exploitation. He endures all suffering but it is only when the atrocities of the capitalists reached the level of brutality that he raises his voice.

Despite the tragic notes of his novels, the ideas of scientific humanism are sustaining and pervasive in his novels. In fact, his consciousness of the need to raise the untouchables, the peasants, the coolies and other suppressed members of society to human dignity and self awareness in view of the apathy and despair in which they are sunk made him a naturalistic humanist.

Humanism means love of man, the whole man with all his weaknesses, instincts and impulses. Humanism means devotion to the concerns of mankind. It is an attitude of mind that concentrates upon the activities of man rather than upon the supernatural world, the world of nature or the so-called animal kingdom. The history of Western humanism goes back to the Renaissance. The Humanism arose as a result of the study of the ancient classics which emphasized things human and of this world in contrast with the medieval pre-occupation of supernatural and life in the other world. Basically, humanism is a Renaissance doctrine, which stresses, the essential worth, dignity and greatness of man. It is in contrast with the older view according to which man was wicked, worthless and doomed to destruction, both in this life and that would come. Renaissance humanists derived their beliefs from the study of ancient poets, historians and philosophers. They believed that man is capable of living a life of reason, dignity, morality and even happiness.

Anand does not seem to have any radically new concept of humanism. He confesses that by humanism he does not mean anything more or less than what it has always meant, illumination or enlightenment in the interests of man, true to his highest nature and his noblest vision.

Anand's humanism follows the concept that the highest reality in the world is man, 'the whole man', and not God and the supernatural. There is no life hereafter and man has only here and now. Institutionalized religion was, therefore, a matter which was best left for individual preference.

Man's highest duty is to realize his full potential for a complete life. This could be achieved by the acceptance of the principles of perfect equality between man and woman, the brotherhood of all men and the right of every person to enjoy social, economic, political and intellectual freedom. The forces that come in the way of achieving this ideal are the various kinds of barriers that separate men- difference in nationality, culture, religion, creed, and caste; the numerous forms of exploitation of man by man, such as capitalism, colonialism, fascism, feudalism, communalism, etc. These forces must be effectively destroyed.

Anand's humanism makes him a novelist with a mission, his mission was to write for the betterment and upliftment of the under-dog of the society. His humanism results from his consciousness of the need to help raise the untouchables, the peasants, the serfs, the coolies and the other suppressed members of the society to human dignity and self-awareness in view of the objectiveness, apathy and despair in which they are sunk.

Anand's humanism, his concern for the under-dog of society reflected in all his novels *Untouchable, Coolie* and the *Two Leaves and a Bud* are significant in this connection. In these novels, Anand deals with the misery and wretchedness of the poor and their struggle for a better life. Almost all his subsequent novels are a variation on the same theme and they bring home to the reader the plight of the over-burdened peasant who is powerless to fight superstition and is baulked at every step in his aspirations for a better life. *Coolie* tells the experiences of Munoo, an orphan from the time he leaves his village in Punjab till he dies of consumption in Simla. *Untouchable* is concerned with the feelings of Bakha, a sweeper boy, and his experiences in the course of a single day in the tour of Bulashah. Both attract the attention of the reader on certain very important social and political problems affecting life in India; So the world of the novels is a microcosm of India. These two novels have served the useful purpose of arousing the conscience of the educated Indians to the problems of untouchablity and economic and social injustice in India.

Anand's aim in *Coolie is* to bring home to the reader, the living conditions of the poor and the heartlessness of the rich and at the same time to suggest that true comradeship of man for man exists only among the very poor people.

Anand's humanism makes him use his art for the service of humanity. Caste and national barriers have no significance for as, he regards all mankind as one. If there is any division, it is that of the rich and the poor, of the have and the have-nots and his purpose is to focus attention on the light of the have-nots, arouse sympathy for them, and thus pave the way for their betterment. Coolies, untouchables, plantation labourers, soldiers at villagers and factory workers are objects of Anand's humanistic attention. He claims originality in being a writer of these men in their immense variety.

Dr. Mulk Raj Anand, through his rare prolificity, bold experimentation and aesthetic sensibility, has made immense contribution to Indian as well as world literature in English. His choice of unconventional subjects and characters has been determined by his Dickensian humanistic philosophy. He set up new trends by introducing negative hero/anti—hero in his novels. His fictional world is peopled by characters from various strata of society- from the lowest to the highest rungs in the hierarchy. Anand has revealed exceptional, psychological insight in the portrayal of these characters who "once were real men and women" and are not mere phantoms of fantasy. However, his otherwise authentic and objective delineation of character is superb which the chief requisite of a work of art is. The present study discusses the oscillation of Anand between his integrity as an artist and his enthusiasm as a reformist.

Mulk Raj Anand, the most prolific and the most widely criticized Indo-Anglican novelist, feels that characters in his novels have been the motivating force- rather the chief cause- behind the writing of his novels. In Anand's novel, it was not the action that decided the choice of characters in his novels. The action instead, was chosen according to the characters he decided to write about. His characters are mostly people who once were 'men and women'. Anand, in his childhood and youth had been intimate with them. He had himself shared their feelings, thoughts, action reactions, troubles and joys. And he had studied their emotions from such close quarters that he could easily identify himself with them. Anand's complete identification with his characters accounts for the remarkable authenticity in their portrayal.

The choice of characters in a novel is determined to a large extent, by the exigencies of the period in which the novel is written and by the writer's own interest, wims, and idiosyncrasies. That is why there is a noticeable change in the concept of hero from time to time. Tom Jones, Moll Flanders and Huckleberry Finn of the early and middle eighteenth century with its love for travelling and adventures gave place to Emma, Elizabeth, and Mr. Bingely enjoying the unperturbed, easy and comfortable life of upper middle class society of the decade of the same century. They, in their own term were replaced by David Copperfield, Oliver Twist, and Nicholas Nickel by fighting the naked and hard facts of life in the nineteenth century. In the modern age with its complexities and interest in psychology, Virginia Woolf and James Joyce rang the knell of the traditional hero and introduced heroes sans heroic qualities. About Indo-Anglian fiction, Williams aptly remarks that "it too seems to have begun with unheroic". Infact, Indian literature in English came to be written when India was engulfed by innumerable and enormous, social, political and religious evils. The nation was under the suppressing yoke of foreign rule. The British rulers subjected the poor Indians to slavish, subhuman existence the rigid class and caste structure of India itself caused intolerable sufferings to people. The exigencies of the situation demanded an exposure of these evils and agitation against them.

The World was unrealistically and hopelessly dismal. To relief the gloom, he provides a ray of hope in the form of these selfless, benevolent, and beginning savior characters. The presence of savior heroes in these novels, according to the Anand, is not intentional, but is a conational to life. About the savior figures he absorbs "actually the saving graces were not created in the novels with the intention to show every time that there is one character that may retrieve the situation. In life there are always such people. And in the presentation of contraries of good and evil, the leafs hope against despair. Despite Anand's assertion that the people like his savior characters are found in life, the fact remains that in the fictional world of Anand, many times these savior characters appear unwelcome intruders. Every often they appear to happen have been forced in the novel with the purpose to preach. They are often used as lifeless instrument to voice Anand message and often they preach the message so overtly that authorial presence is all too palpable. Unable to conceal his purpose in the vile of art, try to "put his thumbs in the scale, which, according to Lawrence is immoral on the path of the novelist.

Anand's choice of characters – both sufferers and saviors –is consistent with his theory of literature and life. Anand has not given a well organized theory of literature, nor does he feel the need of formulating one for writing literature. As Anand absorb "people who say I have no theory of friction are more or less correct. And yet one does not need to formulate a systematic theory to write friction or to react its various impressions, to enjoy its flavors and even to write some criticism of one's own." Anand realizes that the social content of the Indian novelist is different from that of the European writers. He wants that "we have, however, in our newly emergent societies, to understand that we are not the middle classes of Europe and America. we must see our self as we are, we are struggling about the days contempt of the caste order, emancipating our minds from the submission to our man rule, we are dimly becoming aware of nature of our hopeless resignation in the past to the unknown faith, the supreme God Vishnu who will not wake up to help us, because the Kalyug is not yet over." In such a period of transition Anand felt that "the old world was dead and gone, only lingered in the minds of the sentimentalists who always dote on the past. And the ordinary human values, love, justice, beauty, prayer consequently perverted and destroyed. Like Mathew Arnold, Anand felt torn between two worlds- "one dead and the other powerless to be born".

In this period of confusion, Anand felt that one could depend more on art and literature for solace than on religion and philosophy. According to him "literature, music and art are better able to fulfill the needs of our time than religion and beauty is better worth worshipping than God or a Deity for whom the sanctions lie in the institutions of a few mystics." The fact that Anand uses literature as a means to modify society has led critics to dub him as a propagandist, despite his repeated emphasis on the fact that Indian content demands art with purpose. He boldly accepts the negative appellation, as he observes: "All art is propaganda. The art of Ajanta is propaganda for Hinduism. The art of Ellora is propaganda for Hinduism. The art of western novel is propaganda for humanity against bourgeois. Gorky as a humanist dared to speak of man, man's condition, not only to say how awful it is, but he also suggested what man could be. And thus he did propaganda for man." Anand, a great admirer of Gorky's fiction about Squalor and dirt, regards him "the prophet of new literature." And he tries to do in India what Gorky and Dostoyevsky had done in Russia.

Anand's concepts of literature as closely related to life are a by-product of his humanistic ideas. It is his own ardent love for human beings and his pity for the suffering, wretched, downtrodden humanity that lead him to believe that all writers for the sake of man and the function of literature is to enable man recognize his dignity. Anand calls his humanism "comprehensive historical humanism" and discusses it in detail in his *Is There a Contemporary Indian Civilization? Apology for Heroism, Hindu View of Art,* and Prolegomena to a New Humanism" incorporated in Lines Written to an Indian Air with many scattered remarks in his articles, essays and letters. His humanistic faith has been discussed with minute observation by Margaret Berry in the *Mulk Raj Anand: The man and The novelist* and Balarama Gupta in his famous *Mulk Raj Anand: A Study of His Novels in Humanist Perspectives.*

Anand is a "comprehensive historical humanism" because he derives much from the history of Indian religious and philosophical thought and blends it with modern scientific ideas so that his theory achieves universal significance and comprehends the whole of mankind. The traditional values which Anand wants to be operative in modern times are universalism, "intolerant-tolerance" and compassion. Universalism has been inherent in Indian tradition since very remote periods of his history. Anand traces this element in the Vedic hymns in the "simple universal values of mankind, in their worship of nature and their bold speculative outlook about the meaning of creation." Anand is intolerant of orthodoxy and irrational taboos of Indian religious thought, but he is full of admiration for the human values which have percolated through traditional history to modern periods.

Anand is an admirer of humanistic philosophies of Mahatma Gandhi, Rabindranath Tagore and Jawaharlal Nehru. But he does not accept the ideology of any one of them unconditionally. He owes much of his love for the down-trodden humanity to Mahatma Gandhi and his synthetic approach towards the ideologies of east and west to Rabindranath Tagore. He is full of praise for the socialistic pattern of society as preached by Jawaharlal Nehru and stands for his humanism laced with a scientific approach, but he differs from Mahatma Gandhi's capitalistic ideas and from the spiritual sanctions which Tagore and Gandhi find for their philosophies. He wants to strike a combination of Gandhian love for humanity and Marxian gospel of classless and casteless society. He admirers the ethics of Tagore based on a deep study of eastern and western cultures but he does not approve of spiritual sanction in his philosophy.

Anand's humanistic philosophy is sufficient explanation for his choice of characters- the sufferers and the saviors. The sufferers reveal the real plight of contemporary India and the Saviors provide hope against despair. They reveal Anand's existentialism combined with a streak of an optimistic attitude towards life. The relation between the two heroes however differs in various novels. The present study categories my paper on the basis of the relationship between the sufferer and the savior. The relationship depends on the suffering hero's own personality. When he is too passive and weak to fight, a savior figure is introduced from a higher stratum of society. When the sufferer attains maturity of sensibility and strength of mind, he himself fights for the liberty of all those who suffer like him. And when the plight of the sufferer is beyond redemption, and when he is a man of high social profile, no savior character is brought in. In other words, no savior characters are introduced when either the suffering protagonist himself is strong and combative enough to throw a challenge to the iniquitous and suppressive forces of society or when the conditions are so terrible as to be irremediable. In addition there are also some novels in the Anand canon which are fairly free from the shadow of suffering syndrome and therefore have a more disinterested aesthetic dynamic of their own. This study intends to trace the effect of the introduction of the savior characters on the overall aesthetic appeals of Anand's novels.

Humanism in Untouchable

Untouchable is a unique experiment in the art of fiction by its concentration on a single day's experience in the life of its hero. Anand's humanism is brought out at its best in this novel. The hero of the novel is a sweeper boy of just eighteen years of age, a member of the so called untouchable community whose life is nothing but uneventful to an ordinary observer.

A cruel form of slavery perpetrated by a treacherous interpretation of divine intervention in human affairs may be called untouchability. People in India were divided into lower and upper classes of various gradations and each class kept a certain distance from the others. The Brahmins were the priestly class and collaborated with the ruling class or Kshatriyas. The third rank was given to the Vysyas or trading community. The fourth class consisted of the Sudras which included all kinds of menial servants like washer men and sweepers. The last group were prohibited from owning land and kept away from public places and streets. When they walked in the public way they were to shout certain sounds to inform that they were coming so that others will keep distance and avoid being polluted by nearness. These classes were untouchables.

The location of the colony of the outcastes was terrible. The colony of the outcastes was a row of mud walled houses clustered together outside the town and cantonment. It was occupied by scavengers, leather workers washermen, barbers, water carriers, grass cutters and other outcastes from Hindu Society. The ugliness, squalor and misery that lay within the colony made it an uncongenial place to live in.

Anand's *Untouchable* was inspired by the author's childhood memory of a low-caste sweeper boy, who carried him home after he had been injured. The boy was however, beaten by Anand's mother for touching her higher caste son. The novel *Untouchable* was a revelation to readers unaware of the circumstances of life in a caste society and sparked extensive critical debate.

Untouchable narrates a day in the life of Bakha, who suffers a number of humiliations in the course of his day. Bakha is an unclean outcaste, fated by his low birth to work as a latrine sweeper. In the novel Anand presented a powerful critique of the Indian caste system and British colonial domination of India, which has actually increased the suffering of outcastes like Bakha.

The story describes a single day in the life of Bakha, the untouchable belonging to the scavenger caste. The works of this caste was mainly to clean toilets and streets and keep them clean for the upper castes. It was a great pity that the scavenger had to carry the human refuse from the toilets and burn them. No human treatment was shown to people belonging to this particular caste. This caste was considered to be the lower most in the hierarchy of castes in India. They were treated worse than animals. It is shocking that the ancient Hindu society showed such kinds of different treatments.

The treatment that is shown in the town on the arrival of people belonging to this caste seems more human. Bakha has to repeatedly announce his arrival lest a Hindu from the upper caste touch him and get "polluted" (Untouchable, 38). One while walking on the road he did not keep to one side of the road. Someone shouted at him, "Keep to the side of the road, you, low-caste vermin! Why don't you call, you swine, and announce your approach! Do you know you have touched me and defiled me, you cockeyed son of a bow-legged scorpion! Now I will have to go and take a bath to purify myself, and it was a new dhoti and shirt I put on this morning!" (*Untouchable*,38). He is not allowed to come within sixty nine feet of the temple because that would defile the temple. But the sad thing is that he is supposed to constantly keep the premises of the temple clean, by carrying all that is left behind by nature and devotees, the worst of all, he and the people like him are at the mercy of the upper caste people for even basic needs like food and water.

Bakha's story is set over one "eventful" day of his life (Mulk Raj Anand: a Critical Study, 51). Anand beautifully describes the typical day in a small British town neighbouring the soldiers' barracks. The behaviour of the upper caste Hindus described in the novel, churns our stomach. Even the sanyasis are not free from the mentality of the caste system.

The treatment that is given to Bakha is quite in human. Bakha is naturally attracted towards the soldiers who do not treat him as badly as the civilians. He dreams several things. He imagines of being like one of those because for him it is a release out of this terrible world.

One day Bakha overhears someone telling the people about modern toilets, where the human excreta will be flushed out automatically, thereby putting an end to this sub-human activity.

Bakha seems to be a hard-working boy who never disobeys his father despite his dislike for him and his lifestyle. Bakha had worked in the barracks of a British regiment and "had been caught by the glamour of the 'white man's life" (*Untouchable, 2*).

We feel sorry for with Bakha who tried to initiate the Tommies through 'fashion' (*Untouchable,* 2). Bakha is trying to rise above his caste by westernizing yet he receives insults from his friends about his dress. Bakha was interested in imitating the mode of life of the Sahibs. He says, "I will look like a Sahib. And I shall walk like them. Just as they do, in twos, with Chota as my companion. But I have no money to buy things" (*Untouchable 3*). They chide him for dressing like a Sahib and trying to appear to be something that he is not.

Bhangi's are the lowest of the low caste. It is pathetic that they were given jobs more 'menial' and lowly than the other lower castes. They were supposed to clean the latrines and sweep the street. Also they were unable to maintain good hygiene because they are not allowed to access the local well, as their use would render it impure.

Even to highly skilful and intelligent persons also, the treatment was inhuman. However apt and clever a person was at his job, he is not given the permission to rise above his job. Bakha is very dexterous at his skill, saying that he is a bit superior to his job, not the kind of man, who ought to be doing this (cleaning toilets). People said, "What a dexterous workman! A bit superior to his job. Not the kind of man who ought to be doing this" (*Untouchable,* 8).

Despite Bakha's skill and work ethic, he has no chance of moving up in his life. He is forever confined to his dirty demeaning job. Each day Bakha saw the Brahmin boys walk to school and he dreamed of going with them. He wished it would be good to be able to read and write. One could read the papers after having been to school and conversation within the sahibs would be possible.

Education also was denied to the outcastes. Bakha expresses interest in the west by being educated and able to talk with the Sahibs that he would rise above his caste. However he has no chance for education as outcastes were not allowed in school. The parents of the children belonging to superior caste would not allow their children to be contaminated by allowing them to mingle with those of the lower castes.

Bakha's desire to be educated like the sahibs was strong and he offered to pay another boy to teach him to read. Bakha did not have much money. So his offer to pay was indicative of his desire for education. Education was denied to people like Bakha and by becoming educated Bakha hopes to distance himself from the stigma of his caste. Bakha was very much eager to study. One day while standing in the sun he saw a boy dragging his brother to school. A sudden impulse came on him to ask the babu's son to teach him. Bakha says, "Then, do you think it will be too much trouble for you to give me a lesson a day? I shall pay you for it" (*Untouchable*, 31).

A lot of Bakha's actions are motivated by his desire to distance himself from the outcastes. Bakha endures one of the most humiliating and depressing days of his young life in this story. From sunrise he is forced to deal with discrimination, hatred and hypocrisy. He wakes up early morning by his father's shouts. "Get up, ohe you Bakha, you son of a pig, 'Get up and attend to the latrines or the sepoys will be angry" (*Untouchable*, 5).

The first chore of the day is to clean the latrines before the rest of the community gets to use them. When Bakha sleeps in, he is chided by a local Hindu man, who wants to use the toilet. The man says, "Why aren't the latrines clean, you rogue of a Bakhe! There is not one fit to go near! I have walked all around!" (*Untouchable*, 7). Bakha takes this customary abuse in stride and begins to clean the toilets. The local man is thankful for Bakha's work and offers him a hockey stick in a rare display of generosity. He says, "Come this afternoon, Bakha. I shall give you a hockey stick". "A hockey stick! I wonder if it will be a new one!", Bakha thought (*Untouchable*,9).

Bakha is compared to a slave a number of times throughout the book. It is his duty that gives him the energy to keep himself alive. He has been conditioned his outcaste position it is the only one he has had in his life. That is why he takes pleasure when the higher castes compliment him on his job or showed him some other sign of courtesy.

More humiliation is in store for him before his day is out. His curiosity takes him to a local temple, where he climbs the steps to get a glimpse of the wonders inside. Untouchables are prohibited from entering the temple. They were not allowed to see the inside of the temple for purity. Through the window he was interrupted by a priest, who suggested that he was polluting the temple. Soon a crowd gathered and they all beat Bakha saying that they would need to perform a purification ceremony. They scolded him saying that he had defiled their temple. They said that when a temple is polluted it would lead to the destruction of the people. Bakha ran down to the courtyard where his sister was waiting. Bakha heared the little priest scream, "You people have been polluted from a distance. I have been defiled by contact" (*Untouchable*, 53). The worshippers from the top of the steps were shouting,

"A temple can be polluted according to the Holy Books

by a low-caste man coming within sixty-nine yards of it,

and here he was actually on the steps, at the door. We are

ruined. We will need to have a sacrificial fire in order

to purify ourselves and our shrine" (*Untouchable*, 53).

Sohini explained the priest's claim saying "that man made suggestions to me, when I was cleaning the lavatory of his house there. And when I screamed he came out shouting that he had been defiled" (*Untouchable*, 53). Bakha was enraged by this and flees into a rage. This shows the hypocrisy of the other castes in their attitudes towards the untouchables. The higher castes view them as impure, make them do all the menial labour, the idea of impurity is only there when it suits the higher castes' desires.

Hindu Society has degraded to a very great extent in its treatment of lower caste people who worked in polluting and unclean conditions. The people were so much accustomed into such practices that they did not feel personally ashamed by it. In some places the Hindu customs were fascinating and so much irksome that caused misery, humiliation and injustice.

Within his own caste system there were such lot of further subdivisions which made Bakha's life extra hard. It is pathetic to note that despite the fact that India constitutionally abolished the practice of Untouchability in 1950 the practice still continues today and in some cases these people are violently abused. In 1989 India enacted the *Scheduled Castes and Scheduled Tribes (Prevention of*

Atrocities) Act to prevent and punish either state or private abuse against Dalits, to establish special courts for the trial of such offences and to provide for the rehabilitation and relief of the victims.

Bakha suffers several humiliations during the course of a day when he makes two purchases in the town-the red-lamp cigarette and some jalebi (*Untouchable*, 4). On both the occasions when he gives money for the purchase it is placed on a board. They sprinkle water to purity if. They do not receive the money in their hand. They also threw the packets at him. The encounter with a wayfarer is more shocking. The upper caste Hindu charges him with the crime of touching and polluting him. He showers abuses on Bakha. The crowd that gather ill-treat him. This cigarette and Jalebi fall down.

Then comes the greatest shock. The temple priest tries to molest his sister and accuses her of polluting him. They also rebuke him for polluting the temple. In the silversmiths alley he is insulted by a woman who throws bread down to him from the upper storey, and accuses him for polluting her house. Even the wife of Bura Babu scolds him for polluting her son whom he carries home when he is wounded. The wife of Colonel Hutchinson also shows caste prejudice against him.

The intimate friendship between Bakha and his neighbours Ram Charan and Chota is a ray of light in the novel. It is a friendship that goes beyond the barriers of caste for even among the lower castes there is gradation.

Bakha suffers a battle of strong feelings after the discussion of the humiliation with his friends. He thinks of violently opposing the caste prejudice of the upper castes. Chota also wants a corporal punishment of the man who insulted Bakha, Soon Bakha feels that caste prejudice are indeed very strong and it would be totally impossible for him to fight it.

The hockey match that took place between the 31st Punjabis and the 38th Dogras, was indeed, very Pathetic. The Dogras included Bakha, Ram Charan Chota and the Bura Babu's eldest son. As Bakha came to the scene the younger son of the Babu was running towards him. He also carried a new hockey stick. Charan Singh liked the boy for his energy and enthusiasm, but was unhappy that others would not include him in team. Chota was sternly against the boy because he would be a trouble and get injured. The boy said that he would be the referee. Chota objected to that also. The two teams played without any order or system. Bakha was an expert player and scored the first goal with clever movement and strategies. The others said it was a foul and began to quarrel. The captain of the 31st Punjabis team shouted, "Foul, Foul". Chotta responded, "No foul! No foul !" (*Untouchable*, 105). "Throw stones at them, stones", shouted Chota (*Untouchable*, 106). There was a hot struggle between Chota and the captain of the 31st Punjabis. Unable to overcome Chota, the captain and his followers ran away. Chota asked his friends to throw stones at them. One fell on the small boy's head. Bakha lifted the child up and brought him to his house. The boy's mother was angry at Bakha for polluting her son. The elder son told her that Bakha was innocent. Bakha was deeply upset by the event of the injury of the child. It was the stone thrown by Ram Charan that hit the boy. His mother also accused him for touching her child. She shouted, "You eater of your masters, you dirty sweeper! What have you done to my son?" (*Untouchable*,106).

Bakha felt sad that he got only abuse from people wherever he went. People always said that he polluted them and he could not bear the fact any longer. They all say that "Polluted, polluted!" She could have said anything. "It was my fault and of the other boys too. Why did we start that quarrel!? It started on account of the goal I scored" (*Untouchable*, 107).

After this incident Bakha returns home but none show any kindness towards him. His father too was cruel to him. His father said,

"Son of a pig! Illegally begotten! He has no sense of shame! *Play, Play, Play and wonder all day*. As if he has nothing else to do!" (*Untouchable*, 108).

One winter night he was told to go out of his house. Bakha walked for a long time and sat down upon the platform of a *pipal tree*. Then he met Colonel Hutchinson of the Salvation Army. The colonel hoped to drag Bakha into the principles of Christianity. The colonel told him that men are sinners, and Christ saved men from their sins. The Colonel stressed, "I am a padre and my God is *Yessuh Messih*. If you are in trouble, come to Jesus in the *girha ghar*. (*Untouchable*, 115).

"Jesus, tender shepherd, hear me.

Let my sins be forgiven!

Let there be light,

Oh! Shed Thy light in the heart of this boy" (*Untouchable*, 118).

But Bakha felt that he was not a sinner. He felt that to consider oneself a sinner is worse than being treated as an untouchable. Hutchinson wished all people to become Christians, so that there would be no difference between the rich and poor. What Bakha needs and the entire society needs is a change of system and the establishment of a social set up where men are equal, where there is no segregation.

A crowd was waiting for the arrival of Gandhi at the maidan near the Balabash railway station. Bakha listened to what people said about Gandhi. He listens attentively to Gandhiji's speech. Much of it strikes a chord in Bakha's heart. Gandhiji tells the untouchables to stop accepting the kind of inhuman treatment shown to them by the people of the higher castes. He turned to the Harijans and asked them to change their life to gain social acceptability. He wants them to refuse the leftovers of the higher castes. He said that the fault does not lie with the Hindu religion, but those who profess it. In order to emancipate themselves from the oppression of the higher castes, they must purify themselves. They have to get rid of evil habits like drinking liquor. Also all public places must be declared open to the untouchables. This was the only way to liberate them.

Bakha felt that it was a great thing that Gandhiji had done. Bakha thought,

Is he really going to talk about the outcaste, about us, about Chota Ram Charan, my father and me? What will he say, I wonder? Strange that the sahib of the *Mukti* (Salvation Army) said that the rich and the poor, the *Brahmins and bhangis* are the same. Now Gandhi Mahatma will talk about us! It is good that I came. If only he knew what had happened to me this morning. I would like to get up and tell him" (Untouchable, 132).

Mahatma Gandhiji considered untouchability as a great boon. He said,

I regard untouchability as the greatest blot on Hinduism. This view of mine dates back to the time when I was a child" (*Untouchable*, 137). "If there are any untouchables here, they should realise that they are cleaning Hindu Society (*Untouchable*, 138).

Gandhiji also warns the untouchables to reform their character. He further adds,

They should now cease to accept leavings from the plates of high caste Hindus, however clean they may be represented to be. They should receive grain only-good, sound grain, not rotten grain-and that too only if it is courteously offered. If they are able to do all that I have asked them to do, they will secure their emancipation (*Untouchable*, 139).

Bakha was not fully contented with Gandhiji's view. He felt that untouchability is the greatest evil. What is needed is a religious and moral change. Further Gandhiji had told that the untouchables could emancipate themselves by making themselves clean. It was doubtful that if they kept themselves clean, the mind of the upper castes would change. Bakha did not find Gandhiji's philosophy fully convincing.

A young poet had made an interpretation of untouchability, which Bakha found more convincing. Untouchability and caste are interrelated, which can be changed by a revolution in professions. Machines are the only answers. Machines and devices like the flush can free people from doing dirty and degrading work. I wonder what it is like. When the latrines use flush, the scavenger need not touch dirt.

At last Bakha found wisdom in what the man said and wished to get more information about machines that would liberate men like him from dirt and untouchability.

Bakha thought, "That machine, which can remove dung without anyone having to handle it" (*Untouchable*, 146). He further thinks that "I shall go and tell father all that Gandhi said about us and all that poet said. Perhaps I can find the poet some day and ask him about his machine"

(*Untouchable*, 148).

The arrogance and inhumanity of the upper castes find exposure in the novel. The poor people are not looked upon as human beings. The upper caste Hindus do all kinds of things that make the existence of the lower castes difficult. They worship animals like cow and snake and make the monkey shaped Hanuman a God-like figure but they treat the poor people as dirt. The temple itself is a sanctuary of superstition. These people make God also a champion of the case of caste superiority. All the Hindus who come to the latrines are arrogant Shopkeepers, who sprinkle water on the coins and throw things at the lower caste customers are proud.

The novel refuses to accept Christianity and Gandhism as utopian weapons to fight the evil of untouchability. Only a scientific revolution in social and material relations of life can solve the problem. Social gradations are strongly linked to profession. If all professions become respectable, caste feelings will disappear.

Machines and modern systems can alone liberate men from dirty or mean work. If septic tanks and the flush system are introduced, no scavenger will be needed. In other words social revolution is based on scientific revolution and not on religious belief or moral preaching.

Anand belongs to a period in the history of India when the nation was struggling hard to shake off the burden of slavery during struggle was against British imperialism. The Indians were being treated like dogs. The wounds of Jalian wala bagh were not healed. The pattern of responses to the underdog emerges from the humanism of Anand. Humanism is a system of thought in which human values, interests and attitudes are held dominant. It is a kind of love of man with all his weaknesses and impulses. Historically, humanism is a renaissance doctrine which stresses the basic goodness, worth and greatness of man. Anand's humanistic creed has definite features. It is imperative to take a note of Anand's position as a humanist stated by him in Apology for Heroism:

I believe, first and foremost, in human beings, in Man, in the whole man... The humanism which I prefer does not rest on a Divine Sanction... but puts its faith in the creative imagination of man in his capacity to transform himself, in the tireless mental and physical energy with which he can, often in the face of great odds, raise himself to tremendous heights of dignity and redeem the world from its misery and pain... (P: 137)

It is only natural that a creative artist should present his ideas in a framework of philosophy of life which he accepts and advocates. Anand is no exception in this respect. An analytical study of his fictional works reveals that the humanist philosophy has positively influenced Mulk Raj Anand. Thus, in Anand's novels we find that his response to the underdog is primarily human. Although the characters of these novels who suffer and belongs to the lower strata of life and are treated as underdogs by the society yet the motive behind Anand's exposing these people is that they should realize their potential and become the makers of such a world in which they would not be considered as second- rate human beings. An attempt has been made in this paper to trace the responses of Mulk Raj Anand to the class of people who have suffered for a long time and are looked upon by the author as underdogs.

Untouchable is the story of this prolonged indignity and humiliation of this class of society. The opening of the novel strikes the keynote of the theme of the novel:"The outcastes' colony was a group of mud- walled houses that clustered together in two rows, under the shadow both of the town and the cantonment, but outside boundaries and separate from them."(P.11)

Anand has shown convincingly that there is clear line of demarcation within the Indian society. It glitters and sparkles on the surface but houses destructive worms within. The society belongs to the high castes. They are infact, the rulers and keep the low- caste as far away from them as they can. The 'shudras' are meant to perform the lowest of the jobs and are segregated from the main stream of the society. They are subjected to ruthless exploitation at all levels- personal, social, economic, and political. This novel revolves round Bakha who is a sweeper boy. The author has chosen a conspicuous day from his life and through the presentation of the situation occurring on that particular day, he has drawn our attention towards the plight of low caste people. First situation is the pollution through touch of a caste Hindu. It creates a catastrophe. As Bakha walks along the road eating 'Jalebi' and recalling the arrangement he has made for learning English, his gaze is drawn to a woman sitting in a window. He is so deeply lost in his thoughts that he has accidently touched someone passing by. Suddenly he hears,

keep to the side of the road, o he low-caste vermin... why don't you call, you swine and announce your approach: Do you know you have touched me and defiled me, you cock-eyed son of a bow- legged scorpion: now I will have to go and take a bath to purify myself.

The second major situation in the novel is when Bakha's sister Sohini is molested by the priest. The irony in this situation, Anand makes us realizes, is that hue and cry is raised against the molested and not the molester. Thus we see that the holy men who appear in Anand's fiction are corrupt to the core and in their eyes; the lowest of low are quite touchable for the purpose of satisfying their lust. For example, the ascetic in Coolie- he appears as Pandit Surajbhan in 'The Road' seduces a childless woman under the pretext of turning her fertile. Here in Untouchable also, though the holy priest makes unsuccessful attempts to seduce Bakha's sister, the author has exposed the contradiction in the thinking of the so called high- caste people, while a mere touch of the clothes of an untouchable is thought to pollute a higher caste, sexual union is non-objectionable. Sohini raises an alarm to save herself from being molested by the priest Kali Nath but the priest is very clever and extricates himself from the difficult situation by shouting, "Polluted, Polluted". The writer here draws our attention towards the unjust and condemnable behaviour of the so called high caste people who can easily go scot-free by turning the blame on to the suffering, sexually exploited girl. There seems to be a possibility of protest and revenge. But Anand underlines the fact that revolt in such cases is impotent and ineffective. Bakha knows the truth of the whole thing that he finds himself incapable of taking revenge. He returns home crestfallen and shout against the indignities, brutalities heaped by high caste people upon them. The hero's immediate impulse is to avenge the insult but he fails to act. It is here typical treatment of the underdog as given by Anand is projected. The burden of the past, the attitude of the ruling class, and their longing for pity and sympathy crush the will to act. The oppressed underdog in the hero continues and devours him like a monster. He is a total picture of a dog crouching at the door of a banquet hall.

Anand's response could have been blown up in respect of magnitude of the torture, but it remains within the limits of credibility. Anand's early life experience of the company of the children of the sweepers equipped him better to write about them and their sufferings in vivid details. The comment of E. M. Forster in this context is worth recording. He says in the 'Preface' to Untouchable:

Mr. Anand stands in the ideal position. By caste he is a kashatriya, and he might have been expected to inherit the pollution complex. But as a child he played with the children of the sweepers attached to an Indian regiment, he grew to be fond of them and to understand a tragedy which he did not share. He has just the right mixture of insight and detachment, and the fact that he has come to fiction through philosophy has given him depth.

Anand is able to present the darkness in the lives of these untouchable and their suffering with an identity which is extremely sordid and pathetic. Perhaps the subtlest stroke in Anand's portrayal of Bakha's psyche is his account of the untouchable's one dream of life which is not to be a caste Hindu but a white sahib. The sola hat hanging on the wall attracts his attention. He imagines himself clad in a superior military uniform, cleaning the commodes of the sahibs in the British barracks. Bakha has no awe of the Englishman. Although Bakha may look a ridiculous figure as he stumps out in artillery boots, wearing discarded trousers, puttees, breeches and overcoat with "Red Lamp" cigarette between his lips yet it is the manifestation of his inner strength and courage. He thinks that he should imitate the English men because they treated him as a human being where as the native people scorned him for his filthy habits. Bakha's admiration of the sahibs persists right through the book and wanes only when he hears Mahatma Gandhi speaks. These psychic meanderings of Bakha did not change his lot for any practical purposes.

But he had dreamt of a future devoid of the curse of untouchability. As a matter of fact these possibilities have been explored by the author to look for a solution to the problems created by the caste-system in India. He believed in the dignity of man and his work. He believed that caste had nothing to do with greatness of a man he suggests something of the kind of a classless society and these ideas have come to him not from intellectualization of the problem but from his personal experiences. The sensitiveness that he has been able to give to his protagonist in the novel is a felt one. In his portrayal of an individual like Bakha, Anand has convincingly proved that his attitude was humane and he understood the grim realities of this cruel aspect of social life in India.

CHAPTER THREE

Humanism in Coolie

Coolie is one of the most popular novels of Anand. The novel published in 1936 by Mulk Raj Anand gives a clear and poignant description of the poor face of India. It has been translated into over twenty important languages of the world. This been eulogised by readers, scholars and critics alike.

Coolie is one classic example of the story of the underprivileged class of the society and of the oppressed people who cannot even make both ends meet. Its appeal is so much innate, humane potential and wide extensive that has designed it purposive to be translated into more than 38 languages of the world. It has earned for Anand a global reputation as one of the prolific and prominent English novelists. The story is told from the eyes of the narrator and brings to light the inevitable and hidden evils of the Raj, right from exploitation, caste ridden society, communal riots, and police injustice. The novel takes us to different places and cities showing the inhuman and degrading treatment that the poor Munoo gets at the hands of the socially, economically, and politically affluent and higher classes of Indian society and how he copes with all circumstances alone. Anand was able to strike a cord in the hearts of the conscientious Indians with the beautiful and real to life portrayal of the down trodden masses of Indian society, the so called have nots. Mulk Raj Anand was much appreciated and recognized for this novel and was one of those people who were highly influenced by Mahatma Gandhi. And this influence is clearly seen in all his works including *Coolie*. True to his Marxist spirit, he always portrayed the real India, and more specifically the poor India. Though the novel is historically located in 1930s, it continues to enjoy the same contemporaneity in the present century India.

Munoo is the protagonist of this novel *Coolie*. Generally the protagonists of the novels of Mulk Raj Anand are from dirt and dust; they are too meek to report against the evil forces which tend to suppress them and their like. These hero-antiheroes, no doubt, are endowed with certain admirable qualities of the head and the heart; but the cruel, irrational social forces hamper the proper development of these qualities. The diligence, intelligence and sensitiveness of these characters are awfully suppressed that they can never gain confidence to wage a fight for their cause. They, however, do sensitively feel the torture of the unjust practices, but the reaction is limited merely to their acknowledgement of the social status which they are doomed to accept without a hope for emancipation. The knowledge of their helplessness against the establishment, social set-up, traditions, taboos and customs makes them writhe with acute mental agony. They can do nothing but accept their faith.

The summary lines of *Coolie* delineate a bohemian life saga of an adolescent hill boy Munoo. An idyllic life in the kangra hill with friends and relations seemed to be short lived as Munoo's guardian and uncle Dayaram, at the instigation of his irate wife, drags the orphan to town to eke out his living. The orphan boy Munoo runs to avoid every place of cruelty in search of happiness and everywhere he is suppressed. He is aged fifteen and he does various jobs at Daulatpur, Bombay and Simla. He dies of tuberculosis in the end because of poverty. Munoo is exploited greatly in one way or another, by one person or another. Munoo universally symbolizes the suffering of the oppressed and those taken advantage of. Suppression takes major role in *Coolie* to show how pathetic the lives of the Indian people are under the suppressive forces. Through his saga of suppression, Anand shows the decline and upturn in the life of Munoo. Munoo's uncle and aunt consider him as a machine for obtaining money. Munoo willingly receives his role as a slave and agrees to go to town with his uncle. At fourteen, Munoo is forced to work in the house of Babu Nathoo Ram, a worker in Imperial Bank in Sham Nagar. Munoo's romantic views are destroyed by the wife of Babu Nathoo Ram. This lady is not good-natured and always abuses and curses him without any reason. Anand's Munoo is denied happiness. Munoo is humiliated for relieving outside the wall and abuse is showered on him. Munoo suffers physical and mental torture and this shows suppression in the form of child labour. Even at the tender age of fourteen, he is not provided with the basic necessities.

Munoo is, in fact, a burning symbol of millions of unfortunate souls like himself – lost and bereft, abused and down-trodden. If Anand hints at the gradual break-down of the caste system, mainly through the British, in *Untouchable and Road*, he shows in *Coolie* how it is replaced by class system – an evil no less vicious than the former – an awful result of social revolution fermented by the twin forces of industrialism and the cash nexus. Central to Coolie is

Anand's humanistic faith that this class-consciousness born of money or social status can have crushing effects on those that are at the lower rungs. We can see in *Coolie* how the evils of poverty and cruelty crush a bud of youth before it could bloom to any extent. Daya Ram, Mr. and Mrs. Nathoo Ram, Ganpat, Chimta Sahib, and Mrs. Mainwaring too, have only contempt for Munoo. They slap him, kick him, and abuse him. Almost at every turn he comes across only pain and cruelty which make his life a painful saga of suffering. He is forced to become a sort of a purposeless vagabond with apparently no control on his destiny.

By studying all the above characters, we can say the main character, who is Munoo, suffers because he is poor he is a coolie and all other coolies also suffer because capitalists and other rich Indians exploit them physically and economically. Munoo is the representative character in the novel. His longing to live, we can see in the novel. Right from the beginning we can say whether in village or at city, all persons who are responsible for the suffering of the character Munoo are the same. Moneylender seized all property of Munoo's father and his mother. His father died of shock and Munoo became orphan. He worked in textile factory. There also capitalists exploited him. Anand depicted the real condition of downtrodden workers of the society. Anand also shown how a lady exploits Munoo sexually and because of extra work of pulling rickshaw and sexual exploitation, Munoo died. In *Coolie* Anand has shown extreme suffering of the characters like Munoo, Hari-Har and Prabh Dayal.

The novel tells the story of a 15 year old boy who has to work as a child labourer and ultimately dies of tuberculosis. It is the story of Munoo, who is forced to leave his village out of necessity and poverty to work in the city, as a child labourer.It is a great epic of misery which is built on a vaster scale. Its action is not confined to some particular village but moves from the North to the South, and then back again to the North, giving us a cross section of India and Indian Society.

The central theme of *Coolie* is the exploitation of the poor and the under privileged by the forces of capitalism industrialism and colonialism. This theme has been studied in depth with reference to Munoo, a poor helpless orphan, who is denied his fundamental right to life and happiness, who is exploited and made to suffer, till he dies of consumption. And Munoo is not the only victim of such exploitation, the novelist makes it quite clear that such exploitation and denial of life and happiness is the lot of the poor everywhere in India, whether in a village like Bilaspur or small town like Sham Nagar or big cities like Daulatpur and Bombay. The lot of the poor is equally wretched and miserable whether in rural or urban India.

The element of humanism is evident throughout the novel right from the very beginning till the end of the novel. There is the evidence of capitalistic exploitation in rural setting Munoo is met with all forms of exploitation right from the time when he is in his native village. He is quite happy with his playmates. In the idyllic nature surroundings of his native village also, he is ill-treated by his uncle Daya Ram and aunt Gujri. Even this simple rural community is not free from capitalistic exploitation. The victim of exploitation seems to be the terrible destiny of poor Munoo even at this early age. The pitiable fact was that the landlord had seized his father's five acres of land. His father had died a slow death of bitterness and disappointment. A feeling of pity and compassion evoke in our hearts on hearing of his father's death leaving his mother without any source of income.

Munoo's uncle and aunt want him to leave the village, go to the town and make his own living. Aunt Gujri says, "Munoo ohe Munooa oh Mundu! Where have you died? Where have you drifted, you of the evil star? Come back! Your uncle is leaving soon, and you must go to the town!" (*Coolie*, 1).

Munoo was very popular among the boys of his village. Munoo's rival Jaisingh hears that Munoo is going to the town. He asks him "Will you never come back?" (*Coolie*, 3).

Mul Raj Anand was able to strike a chord in the hearts of the conscientious Indians with the beautiful and real to life portrayal of the downtrodden masses of Indian Society, the so called have - nots. This novel is told from the eyes of the narrator and brings to light the inevitable and hidden evils of the Raj, right from exploitation, caste ridden society communal riots and political injustice. The novel takes us to different places and cities showing the inhuman and degrading treatment that poor Munoo gets at the hands of the society, economically and politically affluent and higher classes of Indian society.

The unjust social system makes the denial of the right to life to Munoo. Poverty compels Munoo to be apprenticed to life at the age of fourteen and to be exploited even by his uncle. His only prayer was that he should be given total freedom to live. He is contented with the life there and is happy with his playmates. His first encounter with urban world is in the house of Babu Nathoo Ram, Sub-Accountant, Imperial Bank, Sham Nagar. The lady of the house, Bibi Uttam Kaur a snobbish and suspicious lady under - feeds, nags and humiliates him. Bibiji is short-tempered and swears and curses him more horribly than even his aunt Gujri. Bibiji is never satisfied with Munoo.

She always scolds him for no fault of his. She says,

How shall I carry them! How shall you carry them! How
long shall I have to go on explaining things to you? Hai! We
don't Know that Daya Ram was going to bring such a thick-
headed boy as this. We- (*Coolie*, 24)

The worst thing is that his uncle takes away the three
rupees which he earns. All this, however fail to dampen the
high spirits completely and it is finally this "living vitality"
which drives him away from the house (*Coolie*, 57). At one
day while showing a monkey dance, he bit the daughter of
Bibiji to make the whole thing more realistic. Babu Nathoo
Ram's children screamed in horror and Bibiji bursts out
on a torrent of abuses. Babu Nathoo Ram came in, and
showered blooms after blooms on the poor innocent boy
with a thick stick. He begged for forgiveness but to no avail.
Bibiji scolded him saying, "Vay you eater of your masters!
May you die! May the vessel of your life never float in the
sea of existence!" (*Coolie*, 57).

He could no longer bear the disgrace and humiliation he
had suffered. Bibiji further accused Munoo for biting her
daughter, Sheila. She said,

I am telling you, my heart is burning! This spoiler of our
salt has bitten Sheila on the cheek! Has not the wicked age
come! This boy! He is hardly yet born! And he attacks the
honour of his master's child! Heavens! (*Coolie*, 58).

He slipped out of the house that very evening. He
passed through the bazaars out of the town, crossed the
railway lines, stumbled several times in panic and got hurt.
At last he succeeded in reaching a train. He felt relieved as
the train moved, and cool breeze came in. Finally Munoo
has realized his position in the world. He was to be a slave, a
servant who should do the work, all the odd jobs, someone
to be abused, even beaten.

The Sham Nagar Episode is only the first act in the tragic drama of exploitation. In Daulatpur he is well treated by Prabh Dayal. He considered Munoo as very auspicious. He felt a strong affinity with poor Munoo, for he himself was a hillman from the hills of Kangra. He had come to Daulatpur as an Orphan, and had worked his way up from a coolie in the streets of the city and had become the owner of a large pickle-making and essence brewing factory. Prabh Dayal says, " Strange are the ways of God indeed! He is a very auspicious find. He seems to be from the hills" (*Coolie*, 62).

But his young partner in business Ganpat exploited Munoo. Munoo is

ill-treated by Ganpat who frequently beats him and hurl abuses at his innocent head. Ganpat was jealous of Munoo. He mocks Prabh saying, "Here is a son for you ready-made and complete. And you can forget all about the herbs that you were going to fetch for your wife – or yourself, for I suspect" (*Coolie*, 63).

Ganapat always tries to degrade Munoo in the eyes of Prabh Dayal. He says,

He may be a rogue, a thief. But of course, we need another boy at the works to help Tulsi, Maharaj and Banga, to run errands and do odd jobs. And, it seems, he will be glad enough to have the food, and me need not pay him. And, it seems, he will be glad enough to have the food, and we need not pay him" (*Coolie*, 63).

It is because of his deeds that Prabh Dayal is completely ruined and the pickle factory is sold out. Munoo works as a coolie to make both ends meet. He finds that there is cut throat competition and exploitation in the grain market. The corn traders take advantage of the situation. The coolies are paid extremely low wages and made to carry excessively heavy loads and are abused, beaten and turned out at the least fault, and sometimes merely at the whims of the trader. They are treated as vagabonds and are entirely at the mercy of the forces of capitalism represented by the traders. Munoo is not alone, he is only one out of the countless victims of such exploitation.

Industrial and colonial exploitation is also presented on a much larger and more terrible scale in the Bombay Phase of Munoo's life. In Bombay, poverty and hunger is to be witnessed on even larger scale and Munoo's experiences are even more harrowing. From the struggle undergone by Munoo we can see that the life and hardships of the poor remain the same. The larger the city the more ruthless the exploitation and the greater the human misery. The indigenous pickle factory has now its counterpart in the Sir George white's cotton Mills where the working conditions are even more dreadful. Ganpat has been replaced by the foreman, Jimmie Thomas who is even more tyrannical. The working hours are very long with a Sunday off. The creditors are more numerous and more wicked. When Jimmie Thomas sees Munoo, he asks, " Why did you not bring the whole of your village, you son of a dog!"
(*Coolie*, 173). Hari tells Jimmie Thomas, "O Huzoor, We want to work with you, but be kind and consider our lot. Rice is so dear here" (*Coolie*, 174). The workers were very much at the mercy of their superior employees. The world of the poor remains basically one of hysteria and nightmare; there is the same foul smell and stink, damp and sticky sweat, dust and heat, incense and dung. Sir George White's Cotton Mill is the symbol of western exploitation through its use of machinery, superior technological skill and it obliges the Indian coolies, like Munoo and Hari to work in most unhygienic and suffocating atmosphere for long hours on very poor images, hardly enough to keep

body and soul together. The workers had to reach at their working places at the correct time in the morning. The working conditions were very strict for them. "Time to go to work, the whistle has just gone" (*Coolie*, 181).

The fifth and final act of Munoo's tragedy commences when Mrs. Mainwaring whose car knocks him down, takes him to Simla. She wants a servant so makes him her boy-servant, her rickshaw-puller and there was evidence that he is exploited sexually also. Munoo accepted his lot as a rickshaw-puller. The poor boy is made to work hard, to pull rickshaw uphill for long hours, till his energy is sapped and he begins to cough out blood. At last he passes away in the arms of his friend Mohan, when he is hardly sixteen years of age.

Contact with the British has proved beneficial to the Indians but in several ways, it has also had degrading and corrupting effects. The Indians lose their sense of self-respect and are ready to go to any length to win the favour of their British rulers. The British look down upon the Indians, kick them and insult them. Mr. W.P. England's visit to Babu Nathoo Ram's house was an episode which illustrates Anand's conviction about the exploitation of India by the British Government. Babu Nathoo Ram and his wife were too eager to please Mr.W.P England at their house in order to secure a promotion. By inviting Mr. W.P. England to dinner at his residence, Babu Nathoo Ram hoped to secure his recommendation for his promotion to the post of the accountant in the bank. Babu Nathoo Ram says to Mr. W.P. England, "Well, if you don't care for Indian sweets, Sir then please eat English- made pastry that I specially ordered from Stifles. You must, Sir. Do Please eat something, just a little bit of a thing?" (*Coolie*, 44).

The British Government not only exploited the country's natural resources but also debased the characters of those Indians who were in its service. It created a body of sycophants looking up to the English, becoming a ready tool of exploitation in the hands of their masters. And they lose their sense of humanity and human decency. Nathoo Ram and Daya Ram (and in the next chapter the Todas Mals) have been dehumanized in the service of the English and they have lost all fellow – feelings. This is best illustrated from the way they bully and abuse Munoo.

In *Coolie* humanity is the Centre of Anand's interest. The study of man, the whole man and his life in all its various facets is the concern of Anand. From the very beginning of the novel, we see Munoo trying to forge links with the rest of the world with the other servants in the town of Sham Nagar, and with Chota Babu, and with other children by means of his monkey – dance. He transcends caste considerations. This desire to forge links with the rest of humanity does not admit of even economic or racial considerations Munoo always wanted to play with the children at Babu Nathoo Ram's house. Bibiji had warned the children of the house not to play with Munoo. Sheila tells him, "We don't want you to play with us. Mother said we are not to play with you" (*Coolie*, 57). He desires to be one with the sahibs and with the rich. "Money is everything", he thought. "Money is, indeed everything" (*Coolie*, 55).

Man and his life have been studied in the novel through an exploration of human relationships. Characters in the novel can easily be divided into (a) the oppressed or the poor (b) the oppressors, capitalists, colonialists etc and (c) the wicked or the tools and sycophants of the oppressors and human relationships are determined accordingly.

Study of the relationship between master and servant occupies an important place in the novel. His relationship may be harsh and cruel or it may be kindly and sympathetic based on mutual live and sympathy. In the house of Babu Nathoo Ram Munoo is treated very cruelly. Bibiji makes him overwork from morning till night starves him constantly lashes him with her tongue and he is beaten mercilessly for the least fault. His life in Babu Nathoo Ram's home is miserable and unable to bear it any longer; he is compelled to run away. When Munoo breaks the tea-tray, Bibiji scolds him, "Our house used to be like the houses of the Sahib-logs until this brute came from the hills and spoilt it all. That lovely set of China he has broken, the uncivilized brute" (*Coolie*, 45).

The Kindlier and gentler aspects of servant–master relationship has been studied through the relationship of Munoo with Prabh Dayal and his wife Parvati. His new master and mistress treat him kindly, feed him well and take every possible care of the poor boy. Prabh Dayal says to his wife, "That boy is an orphan. Come we should be kind to him for the sake of religion. We should try to train him to do accounts and things, because he is too good for coolie work. He is intelligent. And let us treat all these boys as one family. There is no harm in doing accounts before Munoo. And the others don't understand" (*Coolie*, 102). This treatment is in sharp contrast with the treatment meted out to him in the house of Babu Nathoo Ram. When Prabh falls on evil days, Munoo tries his best to help him out of his difficulties. He works as a coolie and tries to help him in every possible way. When Prabh leaves Daulatpur he is heartbroken, and he is never able to forget the kindness shown to him by his master. Prabh treats Munoo humanly for he remembers that once he himself was a coolie.

The relationship between the ruler and the ruled, between the colonialists and the colonized get another form of the master servant relationship. The relationship is degrading as it makes the rulers proud and arrogant and the ruled lose all sense of self-respect. There is the policeman who beats Munoo as he works on the railway station as a coolie and the English inspector of police a symbol of British cruelty rather than of British Justice – who has Prabh mercilessly caned for no fault of his. The policeman tells Munoo, "You scum of the earth! You swine, you trickster I will put you in the lock-up......" (*Coolie*, 136). There is also the Englishman who slaps Munoo merely because he had dared to look at his face. The way in which the coolies are ill-treated by Jimmie Thomas and exploited by him is a larger version of the evils of this degrading relationship.

*Coolie*takes us into a world in which comradeship of man for man exists only among the very poorest people. With nothing to hope for their common humanity is all they possess. The relationships between Prabha (at heart still a coolie) Munoo and the other factory employees is humane. The elephant driver, who befriends Munoo and Hari in his inborn sympathy for others, is similar to Prabh. Then there is Ratan, the wrestler coolie. One day an everlasting friendship is developed between Munoo and him. Anand has created the character of Ratan in such a way as to show the comradeship that exists among the very poor. When Hari's hut is washed away by the rains, it is Ratan who invites the whole family over to his place and arranges shelter for them. Ratan tells them,

Ah, yes do come brother. If you can sleep the night with us we can all go together to the factory in the morning.

And then I will present you to the big Mistri Sahib. And we can take a hut near the Mill and you can lodge with us (*Coolie*, 159).

In the novel, Anand has made a comprehensive study of various kinds of human relationships and thus has contributed to the understanding of Man, the whole man. Munoo is a universal figure than life, figure symbolising the suffering and inhuman treatment subjected the down-trodden and exploited masses of India. *Coolie* comprehends the whole of India.

Anand's humanism makes him use his art for the service of humanity. His aim in *Coolie* is to bring home to the reader, the living conditions of the poor and the heartlessness of the rich and at the same time to suggest that true comradeship of man for man exists only among the very poor people.

Coolie is steeped in humanism. It has a tilt towards the poor and the down-trodden. It is a novel of the underdogs. To quote Saros Cowasjee,

It is a study in destitution, or to use peter Quennell's words. "India sees third-class a continent whose bleakness, vastness and poverty are unshaded by a touch of the glamour, more or less fictitious, that so many so many English story tellers, from Kipling to Major Yeats Brown, have preferred to draw across the scene. (The Times of India, December 11, 2003)

Coolie is harshly realistic. It presents a picture of the poor people; their sadness and cruelty, happiness and revolt, exploitation and hunger. From the technical viewpoint of plot and characterization it is certainly not flawless but as a social proletarian novel it is a brilliant success. There is no doubt about it. The typical technique adopted in *Coolie* is naturalistic. Munoo's progress and other things are described in naturalistic setting and prose with 'tantalizing realism,' says Cowasjee. It is the photographic realism that brings accuracy and objectivity and makes the picture very touching. According to K.R.S. Iyengar, there is a Dickensian piquancy of realism in the characters and action of *Coolie*. But Anand shows his grip on the expressionistic also. Expressionistic technique is X-ray photography and it is diametrically opposed to naturalism. It is a technique of bringing out the intrinsic reality or truth of an emotion or situation. Truth can be known only by distortion. Symbols are also used. In the fourth chapter the naturalistic technique of the earlier chapters is replaced subtly by the expressionistic technique. Here Munoo is no longer an individual. He becomes a type like O'Neill's yank in *The Hairy Ape*. The fourth chapter, to use Saros Cowasjee's phrase, is 'Wholly expressionistic in technique and is devoted to dramatizing and universalizing the basic theme-that of the fate of the natural man's essential innocence. *Coolie* is a novel written with a purpose. It is a powerful indictment of modern capitalistic society and its tragic exploitation of the poor. The hero of the novel wants to live. But the society does not allow him to live. He dies of exploitation, poverty and hunger. Humanism is the answer to the problem. If the poor are treated humanely, many of the problems related to them can be solved easily.

Coolie is not merely a piece of propaganda. It is indeed a piece of art. The work is not by a doctrinaire Marxist singing the virtues of the proletariat. Whatever propaganda is found in the novel is 'digested completely.' The speeches detailing the miseries of the labourers and atrocities of employers delivered by the leaders of the Union Congress and Union Jack appear to have been designed and woven by Anand specifically to drive home his point of view since they are all not much comprehensible to Munoo. In this connection the remarks of Saros Cowasjee are very pertinent; "Anand is political novelist. He sees his characters and their actions in relation to India, and often in relation to the world outside India. It is in this that his chief strength lies. At a time when most Indian nationalists thought that Independence would usher in the golden age, Anand saw deeper and asserted that political freedom, without a change of heart, was meaningless. India's present predicament, after twenty five years of freedom, is a vindication of Anand's foresight. What Munoo suffers at the hands of his English Masters in Bombay is no more than what he suffers at the hands of his Indian masters, and even from those of his fellow workers as down-trodden as himself."

As mentioned above, *Coolie* is remarkable for its humanism too. It has given the story of Munoo a human touch. It runs like an undercurrent and saves the novel from being a dark picture of contemporary India. There is a certain philosophical touch and depth. The novel has its shortcomings too. These flaws broadly relate to the structure and plot construction of the novel. The device of the motor accident destroys the probability of its action. It is a cheap romantic device of developing action. Prof.Naik, says that the accident is the beginning of Munoo's end: it is also the beginning of the end of the artistic integrity of the novel.

In *Coolie* we are taken on a guided tour of India, a panorama of the sub-continent from the North to the South on folds itself before our eyes and the degradation and the inhuman treatment of the poor is studied in most varied circumstances and environments. The very spirit of other

India is distilled into the novel. The novel becomes an epic of misery in the real sense of the word. Anand's narrative technique is quite adequate for the task.

Works Cited

Primary Sources

Marak, J.C. 2010. From Literary Naturalism to Hopeful Humanism. Guwahati: EBH publishers.

Anand, Mulk Raj. 1935. Untouchable. New Delhi: Penguin Publications.

Anand, Mulk Raj. 1936. Coolie. New Delhi: Penguin Publications.

Anand, Mulk Raj. 1937. Two Leaves and a Bud. New Delhi: Arnold Publications.

Secondary Sources

Abidi, S.Z.H. *Coolie: A critical study. Bareilly*: Prakash Books, 1998.

Asnani, Shyam M. *Critical Response to Indian English Fiction*. Delhi Mittal Publications. 1985.

Batnagar, Manmohan K., and M.Rajeswar, eds. *Indian Writing in English*. Vol.7. New Delhi: Atlantic Publishers, 2000.

Berry, Margaret (1968–1969). *'Purpose' in Mulk Raj Anand's Fiction.* Mahfil (Michigan State University, Asian Studies Center) 5 (1/2 1968-1969): 85–90.

Berry, Margaret. Mulk Raj Anand: *The Man and the Novelist.* Anstadan: Oriental Press. 1971.

Bhatnagar, M.K. *Political Consciousnes in Indian English Writing*: New Delhi, Babri Publications. 1991.

Bhattacharya, P.C. Indo - *Anglian Literature and the works of Raja Rao.* Deli Atma Ram and Sons. 1983.

C. J. George, Mulk Raj Anand, His Art and Concerns: *A Study of His Non-autobiographical Novels*, New Delhi: Atlantic Publishers, 1994.

Comasjee, Saros.ed. Author *to Critic: The Letters of Mulk Raj Anand.* Calcutta: A Writer's Workshop publications. 1973.

Cowasjee, Saros. So *Many Freedoms: A Study of the Major Fiction of Mulk Raj Anand*, New Delhi: Oxford University Press, 1977.

Daya, B. *Indian Short Story Writers in India: A critical Study. Ranchi: Jubilee* Prakashan. 1985.

Dhawan, R.K.ed. *Commonwealth Fiction in English.* New Delhi: Classical Publishing Company. 1988.

Dwivedi, A.N. *Papers on Indian writing in English.* Delhi: Amar Prakashan. 1991.

Garg, Pramila. *The Freedom Movement in Indian Fiction in English.* New Delhi:Ashish Publishing House. 1993.

George, C.J. *Mulk Raj Anand: His Art and Concerns.* New Delhi: Atlantic Publishers. 1994.

Gupta, G.S. *Balram. Studies in Indian Fiction in English.* Gulbarga:JIWE Publications. 1987.

Gupta, G.S. Balram.. *Mulk Raj Anand: A Study of His Fiction in Humanist Perspective.* Bareilly: Prakash Book Depot. 1974.

Iyengar, K.R.S. *Indian Writing in English.* New Delhi: Sterling Publishers, 1985.

Jai Kumar and Haresh Pandya, "*Mulk Raj Anand*" (*obituary*), The Guardian, 29 September 2004.

Mathur ,O.P. *Modern Indian English Fiction.* Delhi: Abhinav Publications. 1993.

Muller, Herbert J. Modern Fiction: *A Study of Values*. New York: McGram Hill Book Company. 1937.

Murthy, S.Laxmana. "*Bakha: An Existential analysis*". Indian Writing in English. Eds. Batnagar, Manmohan K., and M.Rajeswar. Vol.6. New Delhi: Atlantic Publishers, 1999.

Naik, M.K. *History of Indian English Literature*. New Delhi: Sahitya Academy, 1982.

Naik, M.K.. *Dinensions of Indian English Novel*. New Delhi: Sterling Publishers. 1984.

Narasimhaiah, C.D. *The Swan and the Eagle*. New Delhi: Vision Books, 1999.

Nicholson, Kai. *A Presentation of Social problems in the Indo-Anglian and the anglo-Indian Novel*. Bombay: Jaico Publishing House. 1972.

Orwell, George. *The Collected Essays*, Journalism and Letters of George Orwell – My Country Right or Left 1940–1943, London: Martin Secker & Warburg, 1968, pp. 216–220.

Pandey, Sudhakar, and R.Raj Rao. eds. *Image of India in the Indian novel in English* 1960-1985. Bombay: Orient Longman, 1985.

Patha, R.S. ed.. *Indian Fiction in English: Problems and Promises*. New Delhi: Northern Book Centre. 1990.

Paul, Premila .. *The Novels of Mulk Raj Anand: A Thematic Study*. New Delhi: Sterling Publishers. 1983.

Pradhan, N.S. *Major Indian Novels*: An Evaluation. New Delhi: Arnold Heinemann. 1985.

Prasad, Amar Nath. *Indian novelists in English: Critical perspectives*. New Delhi: Sarup and Sons, 2000.

Rajan, P.K. *The Growth of the novel in India*. New Delhi: Abhinav Publication, 1989.

Rajan, P.K.. Mulk Raj Anand: *A Re-valuation*. New Delhi: Arnold Associates. 1984.

Rao, M. Subba. *Reading in Indo-Anglian Literature*. Vol.1. New Delhi: Kaniska Publishers. 1995.

Sarma, G.P. *Nationalism in Indo Anglican Fiction*. New Delhi: Sterling Publishers, 1990.

Shailaja B. Wadikar, *"Silent Suffering and Agony in Mulk Raj Anand's Untouchable"*, in Amar Nath Prasad and Rajiv K. Malik, *Indian English Poetry and Fiction: Critical Elucidations*, Volume 1, New Delhi: Sarup & Sons, 2007.

Singh, R.A, and VLVN Narendra Kumar, eds. *Critical Studies on Indian Fiction in English*. New Delhi: Atlantic Publishers, 1999.

Singh, R.K. ed. *Indian English Writing*. 1881-1985. New Delhi: Bahri Publications. 1987.

Singh, R .S. *Indian Novel in English. A Critical Study*. New Delhi: Arnold Heinemann. 1977.

Sinha, Krishna Nandan. *Mulk Raj Anand*. New Delhi: Kalyani Publishers. 1995.

Srivastava, Ramesh K., ed. *Colonial Consciousness in Black American, African and Indian Fiction in English*. Jalandhar: ABS publications, 1991.

Varghese , C. Paul. *Problems of the Indian Creative Writer in English*. Bombay: Somaiya Publications. 1971.

Verghese, C.Paul. *Essays on Indian Writing in English*. New Delhi: N.V. Publications. 1975

William, Hyden Moore. *Studies in Modern Indian Fiction in English*. Calcutta: A writer's workshop. 1973.

www.ingramcontent.com/pod-product-compliance
Lightning Source LLC
Chambersburg PA
CBHW061400160726
47995CB00001B/404